The Ultimate Menorca Travel Guide 2023

Memorable for Tourists, Cultural Lovers, and Family Fun

Caradon Jordan

The ultimate Menorca Travel Guide 2023

All rights reserved. No part of this publication may be reproduced, distributed, or transmitted in any form or by any means, including photocopying, recording, or other electronic or mechanical methods, without the prior written permission of the publisher, except in the case of brief quotations embodied in critical reviews and certain other noncommercial uses permitted by copyright law.

Copyright © Caradon Jordan, 2023

The ultimate Menorca Travel Guide 2023

TABLE OF CONTENTS

Chapter One 4
    Introduction 4
Chapter Two 24
    Must-See Tourist Attractions 24
Chapter Three 35
    Immersing in Menorcan Culture 35
Chapter Four 57
    Family-Friendly Activities 57
Chapter Five 80
    Relaxation and Wellness 80
Chapter Six 90
    Conclusion 90

The ultimate Menorca Travel Guide 2023

CHAPTER ONE

Introduction

Welcome to Menorca, a little-known jewel tucked away in the Mediterranean! Menorca is the ideal location if you're looking for an amazing island getaway packed with life-changing adventures. If you're a seasoned traveler ready to encounter new adventures, you'll be mesmerized by the beauty and allure that this island has to offer.

Imagine yourself taking a leisurely stroll along immaculate sandy beaches while the pure waves softly lap at your feet. Menorca has some of the most beautiful coves and bays, luring you in for a leisurely swim or to simply soak up the sun. The underwater environment here is teeming with marine life, providing a captivating display that will leave you in amazement whether you're an experienced snorkeler or just a casual beachgoer.

You will see beautiful landscapes dotted with historic olive orchards and grassy meadows as you go farther inland. The abundance of hiking and exploring options offered by Menorca's natural reserves and protected areas allows you to take in the peace and quiet of nature, breathe in the fresh air perfumed by wildflowers, and see animals in its natural environment.

For those of you who enjoy history, Menorca has a rich cultural past that dates back thousands of years. Explore the ruins of ancient civilizations at historic sites that depict the island's varied past, attractive communities with traditional architecture, and old archaeological sites. The local customs, celebrations, and food exhibit the enthralling fusion of British and Spanish influences, which give your encounter a distinctive taste.

Menorca is a culinary lover's dream, to speak only about cuisine. Enjoy the delicious flavor of just caught fish and indulge in the island's traditional cuisine, which is brimming with Mediterranean tastes. The local markets invite you to immerse yourself in a gastronomic trip that will thrill your taste senses by offering a profusion of fresh food and artisanal delicacies.

Menorca also tempts the daring with a wide range of outdoor activities and water sports. You'll discover excitement and delight in every moment, whether you like sailing along the coast, windsurfing in the energizing air, or kayaking among secret caverns and grottoes.

Small quaint towns and villages strewn around the island provide a glimpse into the slow, relaxed lifestyle of the people for those seeking a more tranquil haven. When you interact with the kind locals, you'll discover that Menorca becomes more than simply a vacation location; it becomes a treasured memory to cherish.

So, if you're a seasoned traveler looking for novel and captivating experiences, let Menorca reveal its secrets to you. Menorca promises an extraordinary trip that will touch your heart and leave you wishing to return time and time again with its varied scenery, rich culture, and kind welcome. Welcome to Menorca, the island where your heart will be stolen!

What Will Make Menorca Unique in 2023

In 2023, Menorca, the jewel of the Mediterranean, will still be a magical and alluring resort. This Balearic Island, which is east of the Spanish mainland, is home to a number of natural marvels, a rich cultural history, and tranquil landscapes that continue to distinguish it as a genuinely unique location. I explored Menorca's distinctive qualities and how it has managed to hold onto its attraction in 2023.

1. Natural Beauty in Its Purest Form: Menorca is well known for its unspoilt, unpolluted landscapes. In contrast to its busier brother islands, Menorca has maintained its allure of nature. With its numerous habitats, including marshes, dunes, and woods, the island is home to a UNESCO Biosphere Reserve, making it a prime location for ecotourism and nature lovers. Menorca's shoreline is surrounded by pure, azure blue seas that beckon travelers to discover remote coves, undiscovered beaches, and secret caverns. The island's dedication to sustainable tourism in 2023 has contributed to the preservation of its natural beauty and ecosystem.

2. Rich Cultural Heritage: Menorca has a long history that has been shaped by a number of civilizations, including the Talaiotic, Roman, Byzantine, and Moorish eras. The architecture, customs, and cuisine of the island reflect this unique mingling of civilizations. In 2023, Menorca will still embrace and commemorate its cultural legacy via a variety of celebrations, including the Sant Joan Festival and the Mare de Déu de Gràcia Festival. Additionally, the Talaiotic ruins offer an intriguing window into the island's ancient past, including Naveta d'es Tudons and Torre d'en Galmés.

3. Calm and Slow Living: Menorca's dedication to responsible development and sustainable tourism has allowed it to continue to be a haven of peace in the Mediterranean. The island's attractiveness as a location where tourists may fully rest and escape the strains of contemporary life is influenced by its peaceful pace of life, friendly residents, and lack of mass tourism. Menorca's commitment to upholding its serene atmosphere in 2023 guarantees that it will continue to be a sanctuary for those looking for a leisurely, introspective getaway.

4. Menorcan cuisine is a delicious blend of elements from the Mediterranean, Spain, and Britain. Food lovers' taste buds are enticed by the island's traditional fare, like Caldereta de Langosta (lobster stew) and Sobrassada (cured sausage). In 2023, Menorca's culinary sector has developed, embracing both its tradition and innovation. An increasing focus is placed on farm-to-table methods and ethical sourcing of regional foods.

5. Outdoor Activities: In 2023, Menorca will provide a wide range of outdoor activities for those looking for adventure. There is something for everyone to enjoy the island's natural delights, from hiking and horseback riding through scenic scenery to water sports like kayaking, paddle boarding, and snorkeling in the crystal-clear seas. Hikers and bikers have a special chance to discover Menorca's rough coastline and stunning vistas thanks to the Cam de Cavalls, an old coastal route that round the island.

The ultimate Menorca Travel Guide 2023

The ideal time to visit

Depending on your interests and tastes, there is no ideal time to visit Menorca.
Summertime (June–August) is the ideal season to visit if you enjoy the beach. The beaches are busy with tourists taking advantage of the warm, sunny weather and waves. But keep in mind that this is also the priciest period to travel to Menorca.

You might wish to think about traveling to Menorca in the shoulder seasons (May–June or September–October) if you prefer a more laid-back beach holiday. The beaches are less crowded and the costs are lower, but the weather is still pleasant and bright.

You might wish to travel to Menorca in the spring or fall if you're interested in its history and culture. You will have more time to explore the island's numerous historical monuments and cultural attractions because the weather is still beautiful and there are less visitors.

Menorca is a fantastic vacation spot for families all year round. Children may play safely on the beaches, and there are many of things to do to keep everyone entertained. However, you might want to avoid going during the summer because the heat might be uncomfortable if you have young children.

Here is a more thorough explanation of when visitors of various sorts should go to Menorca:

Beachgoers: from June to August

lovers of culture: spring or autumn

Families: All the time

Cycling and hiking season: spring or fall

Birdwatchers: April through June and September through October

Drinkers: September to October

You will have a great time in Menorca whenever you decide to travel there. Everyone can find something to enjoy on the island, including families, culture vultures, and sunbathers.

Visa requirements

As long as they are visiting Menorca for fewer than 90 days, nationals of the majority of nations do not require a visa to do so. Citizens of the United States, Canada, Australia, the United Kingdom, and the majority of European nations are included in this. There are a few exceptions, though, so it's best to confirm with your neighborhood Spanish embassy or consulate.

If a visa is required, you must apply for one at the Spanish embassy or consulate in your country of residence. It is necessary to verify with the embassy or consulate for precise criteria as the application procedure might differ based on your nationality.

Requirements for passports

Your passport must still be valid at least three months after the day you want to leave Menorca. Additionally, it must include a minimum of two blank pages for stamps.

Other Conditions

When traveling to Menorca, you must have the following items in addition to a current passport and visa (if necessary):
Tickets for round-trip or subsequent flights
evidence of accommodations
Medical travel insurance
enough money to pay your stay
Health conditions
No particular health conditions are necessary to visit Menorca. But it's always a good idea to be up to date on your immunizations, especially if you're coming from a place where yellow fever is a big problem.

Options for Accommodation
Accommodation for tourists
Hotels: Menorca offers a wide range of lodging alternatives, from opulent resorts to more affordable inns. The time of year, the area, and the facilities all affect hotel pricing.
Apartments: Visitors to Menorca often choose to stay in apartments. Apartments provide greater room and privacy than hotels and can

be rented by the week or the month. The cost of an apartment varies according to its size, location, and amenities.

Villas: Families and groups of friends should consider staying in villas. Apartments lack the room and seclusion that villas have, and they also frequently lack gardens and swimming pools. The cost of a villa varies according on its size, location, and amenities.

campsites: Menorca has a few campsites, which are a fantastic choice for vacationers on a budget. The location and facilities of a campground affects the cost.

Cultural Adjustment

Hostels: For tourists on a tight budget who wish to socialize, hostels are a terrific choice. In addition to individual rooms and shared dorms, hostels frequently contain a common kitchen and living room. Prices for hostels vary based on facilities and location.

Bed & breakfasts: For tourists looking for a more intimate encounter, bed and breakfasts are a terrific choice. Private rooms are available, breakfast is provided, and bed and breakfasts frequently have a quaint ambience. The cost of a bed and breakfast varies according on the facilities and location.

Farmstays: If you want to see rural Menorca, a farmstay is a fantastic alternative. Farmstays provide lodging on active farms and frequently provide recreational pursuits like bicycling, hiking, and culinary workshops. Prices for farm stays vary according on location and amenities.

Accommodation for Families

Hotels that welcome families: There are several family-friendly hotels in Menorca that include features like kids' clubs, playgrounds, and swimming pools. The cost of family-friendly hotels varies according on facilities and location.

Apartments: Families may stay in apartments in Menorca as well. In comparison to hotels, apartments provide greater room, privacy, and are frequently equipped with kitchens, which is beneficial for families with small children. The cost of an apartment varies according to its size, location, and amenities.

Villas: For families that need more room and solitude, villas are a fantastic alternative. Families with young children will love the fact that villas frequently have their own garden and pool. The cost of a villa varies according on its size, location, and amenities.

The price of lodging in Menorca varies according on the season, the area, and the kind of lodging. In general, the peak seasons (July and August) will cost you more for lodging than the shoulder seasons (May, June, September, and October).

The breakdown of the typical nightly price of lodging in Menorca is as follows:

Cost: €50 to €100

Between €100 and €200

Luxury: above €200

Menorca's transportation system
The island, which is a well-liked vacation spot, has an advanced and effective transportation system that enables inhabitants and visitors to explore its many landscapes, historical monuments, and lovely villages. This will give a rundown of the several modes of transportation that are offered in Menorca while emphasizing essential features of each one.

1. Airport
The major entry point to the island is Menorca Airport (Aeropuerto de Menorca), which is located 4.5 kilometers (Mao) southwest of Mahón. Tourists from other nations may easily reach Menorca thanks to the airport's local and international airline service, which links Menorca to important cities around Europe.

2. Commuter Bus Services

The Transport Consortium of Menorca (Consorcio de Transportes de Menorca), which runs the island's public bus system, offers an affordable and dependable means to go between cities and popular tourist attractions. The air-conditioned, contemporary buses provide customers with relaxing trips. They connect well-known locations like Ciutadella, Mahón, and several smaller communities and run on set itineraries.

The majority of the island is covered by a variety of routes. Although buses are a less expensive alternative than cabs, they are not as frequent. For one trip, the cost is €1.40 for adults and €0.70 for kids. Additionally, day tickets and weekly passes are offered.

3. car lease

Tourists frequently choose to rent a car in Menorca because it gives them the opportunity to explore the island at their own speed. There are several automobile rental companies with a variety of vehicles to fit various demands and price ranges at the airport and in main cities. It's significant to note that prior reservations are advised to obtain the preferred car during the busiest travel season.

If you want to see the island at your own speed, renting a car is a fantastic alternative. On Menorca, there are several different vehicle rental agencies, making it possible to compare costs and choose the best offer. An average day's automobile rental costs about €40.

4. Taxis

In Menorca, taxis are widely accessible and a practical choice, especially for short distance travels or when venturing off the beaten bus path. In large cities, tourist hotspots, and airports, you may find them at taxi stands. To guarantee equitable pricing for passengers, taxis are metered and their charges are controlled by the local government.

They may be hailed on the street or reserved in advance, and they are reasonably priced. The base cost is 2.40 euros, and the per-kilometer fare is 1.20 euros. Each additional piece of baggage will cost you €0.70.

5. Bicycles and Scooters

Renting scooters or bicycles is a great choice for people looking for a more adventurous way to see Menorca. Scooters, mopeds, and bicycles are frequently available for rent at rental businesses, allowing guests to take in the gorgeous coastal roads and landscapes while breathing in the clean sea air.

Renting a scooter is a fun and inexpensive way to move about Menorca. Scooters are simple to use and may be hired at many locations over the island. Scooter rentals often cost roughly €20 per day.

6. Ferry and Boat Services

Due to the island's location, Menorca relies heavily on boat and ferry services for transportation, especially when it comes to reaching certain beaches, coves, and adjacent islands. Regular ferry service connects Menorca with Mallorca and other surrounding Balearic Islands. Tourists may also take boat trips to explore the breathtaking coastline and undiscovered attractions nearby.

7. Cavalls, Camilo

The Cam de Cavalls is a 185-kilometer-long, historic coastal road that surrounds the whole island. The walkway, which the British initially utilized as a defensive system, is today a well-liked hiking and biking route that lets travelers get up close and personal with Menorca's natural beauty and ancient monuments.

Concerns about the environment and sustainability

Sustainability and environmental considerations are of the highest significance given the rising number of tourists visiting Menorca each year. To minimize carbon emissions and protect the island's natural beauty, local governments and companies are trying to establish eco-friendly transportation choices, promote electric or hybrid automobiles, and promote the use of public transit and bicycles.

CHAPTER TWO

Must-See Tourist Attractions

Menorca, a tranquil and lovely island in the Mediterranean Sea, attracts tourists from all over the world with its plethora of enthralling tourist attractions. Menorca is a popular tourist destination because of its pristine scenery, beautiful seas, extensive history, and distinctive cultural heritage. Following are a few of Menorca's must-see attractions, which range from gorgeous beaches and historical landmarks to quaint villages and environmental preserves:

1.Ciutadella de Menorca

The lovely town of Ciutadella, which served as Menorca's previous capital, is home to many ancient sites and winding cobblestone alleyways. While the gorgeous port welcomes visitors to take leisurely strolls and discover nearby eateries, the great Cathedral of Menorca, which dates to the 13th century, stands as an astonishing architectural marvel. Plaça des Born, the attractive town square, is a hive of activity, surrounded by lovely structures and busy eateries.

Ciutadella de Menorca may be contacted by any of the following:
Call City Hall at (971) 381 050.
Call the office of tourism at +34 971 382 693.
Airport: +34 971 382 000, Hospital: +34 971 382 000, Police: +34 971 382 000, and Fire Department: +34 971 382 000

2.*Mahón (Maó)*
Mahón, the capital of Menorca at the moment, is a bustling city with a large natural port. Enjoy the stunning views of the Mediterranean while strolling along the coastline. The greatest way to appreciate the city's architectural splendor is to go around the old town, where ancient structures and houses reflect Menorca's varied cultural influences. Visit the Menorca Museum, which

has an interesting collection of objects spanning the island's history, as soon as possible.

There are a lot of sights and activities in Mahon, but these are some of the best:
The Cathedral of Santa Mara, the Castle of San Felipe, and the Plaza de Espaa are just a few of the historical and cultural landmarks that can be found in Mahon's Old Town, which is a UNESCO World Heritage Site.

Visit the Natural Harbor: One of the world's largest natural harbors, the Natural Harbor of Mahon is a well-liked location for fishing, sailing, and swimming. For a different view of the city, you may also take a boat tour around the port.
Take a stroll or a bike ride along the shore: Mahon's waterfront is a terrific area to exercise. You may take in the waterfront vistas and perhaps even get a glimpse of some dolphins or whales.

Visit the Museum of Menorca: The Museum of Menorca is a fantastic resource for learning about the island's past and present. It has a variety of items dating from the Paleolithic era to the present.

3. *Cala Macarella and Cala Mitjana*

Cala Mitjana and Cala Macarella are two of Menorca's most gorgeous beaches, which are known for being among the best in the world. These lovely coves are ideal for swimming, snorkeling, and sunbathing because of their fine white sands and transparent turquoise seas. Visitors may get a taste of paradise thanks to the surrounding cliffs and rich vegetation that add to their natural charm.

The most visited beaches on Menorca are Cala Macarella and ala Mitjana. They are situated 15 kilometers south of Ciutadella in the southern region of the island. The beaches are a well-liked tourist attraction since they are surrounded by steep cliffs and have pristine water.

To travel to Cala Mitjana and Cala Macarella, there are various options. The simplest method is to catch a bus from Mahón or Ciutadella. A parking park where the bus stops is about a 10-minute walk from the beaches. The beaches may also be reached by car; however parking spots are scarce.

4. Naveta d'es Tudons

One of Menorca's most notable historical landmarks is Naveta d'es Tudons, an old megalithic burial site from the Bronze Age. The noteworthy illustration of the island's prehistoric past is the unusual tomb building, which is built like an upside-down boat. The importance of the site and the knowledge supplied by the on-site exhibits will attract visitors interested in archaeology and history.

5. S'Albufera Natural Park in Grau

The S'Albufera d'es Grau Natural Park should not be missed by nature lovers. The many habitats of Menorca, including wetlands, marshes, and sand dunes, are displayed in this protected area. The abundance of migratory and local bird species makes it a sanctuary for birdwatchers. Additionally, there are hiking routes that take visitors to serene beaches and breathtaking vistas.

S'Albufera d'es Grau is situated in the towns of Maó and Es Mercadal in the east of Menorca. S'Albufera d'es Grau Ctra. Maó-Fornells, km 6,5 07760 Maó, Menorca, Spain is the precise address.

Public transit is a viable option for getting there. "Es Grau" is the name of the closest bus stop, and it is situated on the Me-7 route. About 25 minutes pass by on the bus from Maó, and about 45 minutes pass on the bus from Ciutadella.

You may bike or walk to the park's entrance from Es Grau. The park's hours of operation are from 9:00 AM to 5:00 PM every day, and admission costs €5 for adults and €2.50 for kids.

6. Monte Toro

Monte Toro, the island's highest point, provides sweeping views of Menorca's gorgeous topography. A monastery honoring the Virgin of El Toro at the peak offers a sense of peace and serenity. There are various pathways leading to the peak for hikers, allowing them to interact with the island's natural beauty as they go.

7. La Mola and La Mola de Menorca Fortresses

Fortresses The historical military installations La Mola and La Mola de Menorca were built to protect Menorca. La Mola, a military engineering marvel with underground passages and a maze of rooms to explore, is located in Mahón's bay. On the opposite side of the island, La Mola de Menorca provides expansive views of the coastline and the opportunity to discover the island's historical strategic importance.

8. Fornells

Fornells is a little fishing community well recognized for its top-notch seafood restaurants and other water sports. This charming village is the ideal location to sample Menorca's delectable cuisine, including the well-known lobster stew. In addition, visitors may take advantage of the protected bay's sailing, windsurfing, and kayaking opportunities or go on a boat excursion to see the adjacent islands and caverns.

9. Cap de Cavalleria

Cap de Cavalleria, Menorca's northernmost point, is a craggy and alluring headland with breathtaking cliffs and enchanting sea vistas. A great location to view the spectacular Mediterranean sunsets is from the lighthouse at the cape. Following the coastal routes will allow hikers to find secret coves and unusual rock formations.

10.*Binibeca Vell*

A classic Mediterranean village, Binibeca Vell is a beautiful and scenic fishing community. Its tiny squares, whitewashed houses, and winding lanes give the area a picture-postcard appearance. Visitors may enjoy the neighborhood beach for a leisurely day by the sea while exploring the hamlet, which is like traveling back in time.

Menorca's Natural Wonders and Nature Reserves

Off the coast of Spain, in the Balearic Sea, sits the little island of Menorca. It is renowned for its gorgeous beaches, pure seas, and breathtaking natural surroundings. The island is also home to a number of natural marvels and reserves where a vast range of plant and animal life may be found.

Natural Park of S'Albufera des Grau

One of the most well-known natural preserves in Menorca is the Parque Natural de s'Albufera des Grau. A variety of habitats, including marshes, lagoons, woodlands, and beaches, may be found there. It is situated in the northeast of the island. More than 200 different bird species may be found in the reserve, along with a variety of other creatures including rabbits, foxes, and deer.

The following address is in Es Grau, Illes Balears, Spain: Ctra. Es Grau, Km.
Dial +34 971 354 500.

Cavalls, Cami

Long-distance trail called the Cami de Cavalls encircles the whole island of Menorca. It is a well-liked track for bicycling and trekking and provides breathtaking views of the island's coastline. Beaches, cliffs, woods, and farming are just a few of the diverse environments that the path traverses.
Phone: +34 971 365 000

Address: Cami de Cavalls, Menorca, Spain

The Cala Pregonda

Northwest of Menorca is where you can find the lovely bay of Cala Pregonda. It is renowned for its cliffs, turquoise seas, and white sand beaches. The cove is a well-liked location for kayaking, swimming, and snorkeling.

Contact information: Cala Pregonda, Menorca, Spain +34 971 354 500

Turqueta Beach

In Menorca's northwest is Cala Turqueta, another stunning cove. White sand beaches, blue seas, and pine trees are its most famous features. The cove is a well-liked location for sunbathing, swimming, and snorkeling.

Contact information: Cala Turqueta, Menorca, Spain +34 971 354 500

CHAPTER THREE

Immersing in Menorcan Culture

Being fully immersed in Menorcan culture offers a singular and engaging experience, allowing visitors to explore a world of customary celebrations, cuisine, handicrafts, and the island's interesting history. This detailed essay tries to emphasize the numerous components of Menorcan culture, offering a thorough manual for anyone wishing to comprehend and accept the island's distinctive personality.

1. Understanding the historical background of the island is crucial for understanding Menorcan culture. Menorca has had a wide range of civilizational influences over the years, including those from the Talayotic, Roman, Byzantine, Moorish, and British periods. The island's architecture, practices, and traditions bear the unmistakable imprint

of each of these civilizations, producing a rich and fascinating cultural tapestry.

2. Festivals and Traditions: The most well-known event takes place in Ciutadella, the island's historic capital, during the final week of June. Menorca is noted for its colorful and energetic festivals, known as "Festes de Sant Joan." The "Jaleo," a Menorcan horse dance performed on its hind legs while being ridden through the city's winding alleys, is the centerpiece of this festival. The "Cavallers" (horsemen), "Cossiers" (dancers), and "Fabioler" (flagbearer) are further historic components that each lend to the festival's distinctive charm.

Attending one of the various festivals or events held on Menorca is among the greatest ways to explore its culture.

Seasonal Festivals

In Menorca, the summer months are a time for festivities. Festivals are conducted in cities and villages all around the island. The Fiestas de Sant Joan, which take place in Ciutadella in June, are the most well-known of these celebrations. These celebrations, which are a riot of color, music, and dancing, honor Saint John the Baptist's feast day.

Various more well-liked summertime events in Menorca include:

- Es Castell's Sant Jaume celebrations in July
- Sant Cristfol celebrations at Es Migjorn Gran (July)

- August brings Sant Gaietà celebrations at Llucmaçanes.

- Sant Llorenç celebrations at Alaior (August)

- Sant Climent's Sant Climent Fiestas (August)

- Ferreries hosts Sant Bartomeu celebrations in August.

- Sant Llu's Sant Llu's Fiestas (September or August)

- Maó's La Mare de Deus Gracia Festival (September)

3. Gastronomy: Traditional Menorcan dishes include "Caldereta de Langosta," a delightful lobster stew, and "Tumbet," a vegetable casserole. "Queso Mahón," a distinctive local cheese, is a must-try for cheese enthusiasts. Moreover, Menorca's well-known "Pomada," a cool drink made from local gin and lemonade, is a popular choice during the sweltering summer.

Here are some of the most popular Menorcan specialties, along with recipes and preparation instructions:
Langosta Caldereta
Menorca's most well-known dish is called caldereta de langosta, and it is a must-try for

any visitor to the island. The lobster is the star of the show and should be fresh and cooked until it is tender in this tomato, onion, garlic, and parsley stew that is traditionally prepared in a terracotta pot.

Recipe:

Ingredients:

1.5 pounds of live lobster.
Olive oil, 1 tbsp
one sliced onion
2 minced garlic cloves
1 (28-ounce) can of whole, peeled, and manually crushed tomatoes
half a cup of dry white wine
14 cup finely minced fresh parsley
pepper and salt as desired

Instructions:

Bring water in a big saucepan to a boil.
Cook the lobster for 5 minutes after dropping it into the hot water.
The lobster should be taken out of the water and given some time to cool.

Largely cut the lobster flesh after removing it from the shell.
Over medium heat, warm the olive oil in a big saucepan.
Cook the onion and garlic in the saucepan for 5 minutes or until tender.
To the saucepan, add the tomatoes, wine, and parsley.
The mixture should be brought to a boil before being simmered for 30 minutes on low heat.
Cook the lobster flesh for an additional 10 minutes after adding it to the saucepan.
To taste, add salt and pepper to the food.
Serve warm.

Ensaimadas

Traditional pastries from Menorca are called ensaimadas, and they are a delightful way to start the day. Yeast dough is used to make them, and sweet or savory contents like custard, cheese, or meat are then added. Although they can also be prepared in a conventional oven, ensaimadas are typically baked in a wood-fired oven.

Recipe:

Ingredients:

1 cup of warm (between 105 and 115 °F) water

two tablespoons of dried active yeast

1 teaspoon of sugar

1 salt shakerful

Olive oil, 1/4 cup + more for grating on the bowl

3 cups of all-purpose flour, plus additional amounts for dusting the workspace

Filling:

1 cup of the sausage, cheese, or custard filling

Instructions:

Mix the yeast, sugar, and warm water in a large bowl. Let it sit for five minutes until the yeast begins to foam.

Add the salt, extra virgin olive oil, and two cups of the flour. Until a dough forms, stir.

Knead the dough for 5-7 minutes until it is soft and stretchy. Place the dough on a lightly floured surface.

Use olive oil to coat a large bowl. Turn the dough in the basin to coat it with the oil.

Put the dough in a warm spot and let it sit for an hour or until it has grown to twice its original size. Make sure to cover the bowl with plastic wrap.

Divide the dough in half after punching it down.

Roll each half of the dough into a 12-inch circle.

Overlay the dough circles with the filling.

From the center to the outside, wrap up the dough rounds like a jelly roll.

To seal the dough, pinch the ends together.

On a baking sheet covered with parchment paper, arrange the ensaimadas.

The ensaimadas should rise for 30 minutes, or until doubled in size, in a warm environment. Put some plastic wrap over the baking sheet.

Set the oven to 350 degrees Fahrenheit.

Ensaimadas should be baked for 20 to 25 minutes, or until golden brown.

Prior to serving, allow the ensaimadas to cool off on a wire rack.

Sobrasada

A cured sausage called sobrasada is produced from pig belly and shoulder. It is usually smoked over oak wood and seasoned with salt, garlic, and paprika. Popular in Menorcan cooking, sobrasada can be consumed on its own, spread over bread, or added to other recipes.

The following components are needed to produce your own sobrasada:

100 grams of ground pork

paprika, half a cup

1 teaspoon of salt

Black pepper, 1 teaspoon

1 teaspoon of powdered garlic

1/8 teaspoon cumin powder

Instructions:

Combine all of the ingredients in a big bowl. Blend well.

Put the mixture inside a casing for a sausage.

Give the sausage at least three months to cure.

The sausage is ready to eat once it has been cured. For up to two weeks, sobrasada can be kept in the refrigerator.

Here are some well-known eateries in Menorca, along with their addresses and phone numbers:

Sa Nacra Restaurant

The following address is in Ciutadella de Menorca, Illes Balears, Spain: Carrer del Portal de Ses Taules, 1, 07760

Contact number: +34 971 38 35 24

url of the website: restaurantsanacra.com/es

In a cave with a view of Ciutadella's bay, this restaurant is situated. It offers typical Menorcan seafood meals including caldereta de langosta and arroz de la tierra (rice cooked in pottery).

S'Amarador Ciutadella of Menorca Restaurant

The following address is in Ciutadella de Menorca, Illes Balears, Spain: Carrer del Port, 16, 07760

Contact number: +34 971 38 35 24

Website address: samarador.com

This eatery boasts a balcony with views of the port and is also situated in Ciutadella. It offers a selection of grilled meats and veggies in addition to seafood meals.

Smoix Dining Room

The following address is in Ciutadella de Menorca, Illes Balears, Spain: Carrer del Carme, 10, 07760

Contact number: +34 971 38 28 08

Website address: www.smoix.com

This eatery features a contemporary and minimalist décor and is situated in Ciutadella's old town. It offers cuisine produced with local, fresh ingredients that are seasonal.

These are just a few of Menorca's numerous excellent eateries. Try the caldereta de langosta, arroz de la tierra, or oliaigu if you're seeking for authentic Menorcan food. Smoix Restaurant is a terrific choice if you're searching for something a little more contemporary.

You might also wish to try the following other well-known delicacies while visiting Menorca: Local white cheese prepared from cow's milk is called queso de Mahón. It frequently comes with fruit or honey.

Fish meatballs are a well-liked hors d'oeuvre or snack. They are prepared using a combination of fish, bread crumbs, and seasonings.

Rice that has been cooked with vegetables, meats, and sausages is known as arroz de la Tierra. It is a warming meal that is ideal for a chilly day.

Popular tapas items include cured sausages. They are prepared with herbs, spices, and pork.

In tumbet, potatoes, tomatoes, eggplant, and peppers are used to make a vegetable stew. This traditional Menorcan dish is excellent for a summer lunch.

Lobster, tomatoes, onions, and spices are used to make the lobster stew known as caldera de langosta. It's a meal that's rich and savory and ideal for a special occasion.

4. Arts & crafts: Traditional workmanship is highly regarded on Menorca, where there is a strong artisan community. Beautiful products like "Avarcas," the island's well-known leather sandals, and "Sobrasada," a hot cured sausage made from pork, are manufactured by talented craftsmen. Another outstanding example of the island's artistry is the "Taula," an ancient megalithic structure that is exclusive to Menorca and demonstrates the technical prowess of the prehistoric inhabitants.

Pottery (Olis de Menorca): For many years, Menorca has been a center for the production of pottery. A variety of ceramic objects are made from the red and black "marès" clay found on the island. Vases, plates, bowls, and tiles for decoration are made using conventional methods including the potter's wheel and hand modeling. Prices for Menorcan ceramics range from €20 to €200 for minor things and up to €500 for bigger and more intricate pieces, depending on the size and complexity of the work.

Menorca Pottery Crafts Contact Information
Center for Menorcan Artisans:
the third floor of Carrer Sant Francesc in Mahón
Contact number: +34 971 36 45 45

The Menorquin:
Carrer Isabel II, 11 in Ciutadella is the address.
Contact number: +34 971 38 02 02
The Gall Tower

In Es Castell, at 7 Carrer Sant Jaume.
Contact number: +34 971 34 15 55

Leatherwork (Treballs de Talaiot): Skilled artisans still work with leather to produce a variety of goods, including shoes, belts, bags, and accessories. The art of leatherworking in Menorca dates back to the Talaiotic period, a prehistoric era characterized by stone structures known as "talaiots." Leathercraft from Menorca is famous for its superior quality and robustness. Belts and other minor leather items typically cost approximately €50, but elaborately crafted bags and shoes can cost anywhere from €150 to €500 or more.

Address and phone number
Lin Marqués, from Menorca, Artesania
The following address is in Ciutadella de Menorca, Illes Balears, Spain: Carrer Sant Francesc, 27, 07760
Contact number: +34 667 42 01 34

Menorca Artisanal Center
Place of business: Carrer Llus Bosch i Alsina, 8, 07730 Es Mercadal, Illes Balears, Spain
Contact number: +34 971 15 44 36
MENORCA'S SON BOU SCUBA
Location: 10, Carrer Punta Prima, Son Bou, Illes Balears, Spain (70760).
Dial +34 696 62 82 65.

Advice on purchasing leather goods in Menorca
Selecting a trustworthy store or craftsman is crucial when purchasing leatherwork in Menorca. As a result of the prevalence of fake leather products on the market, caution is advised.
Search for leather that is supple and soft. Leather that is of high grade will be smooth to the touch and spotless.
Inquire with the vendor about how to take care of the leather items you're interested in. With the right maintenance, leather of good

quality ought to be able to tolerate frequent wear.

Textile Weaving (Tèxtils Menorquins): Another ancient craft practiced in Menorca that has been passed down through the years. Skilled craftspeople produce exquisite textiles and clothing from locally obtained materials like wool and cotton. The "abarcas," or traditional Menorcan sandals made of braided leather and jute, are the island's most well-known export. The intricacy and level of skill of a Menorcan textile's component parts determine its price. A typical pair of abarcas costs between €40 and €80, whereas handwoven items like scarves and shawls can cost anywhere between €30 and €150.

Jewelry (Joieria Menorquina): The history and natural beauty of Menorca are reflected in the jewelry-making process. Craftsmen produce elaborate creations using metals like silver and gold that are influenced by the sea, nature, and conventional themes. Menorcan jewelry is widely prized for its originality and meticulous craftsmanship. Menorcan jewelry costs vary according on the quality of the materials, the complexity of the design, and the reputation of the maker. Simple silver jewelry may cost as little as €30, while exquisitely designed gold jewelry may cost as much as €200.

Visit the Centre Artesanal de Menorca at Es Mercadal if you're interested in learning more about jewelry art production in Menorca. This facility offers a modest shop where you may buy goods created by regional artists in addition to a permanent exhibition of jewelry and other handicrafts.

Here are a few of the Menorcan jewelers:
The owner of S'agoa Jewelry, artist Sagrario Costa, crafts magnificent and one-of-a-kind pieces of gold and silver jewelry. She draws inspiration for her designs from Menorca's natural beauty and frequently incorporates seashells, coral, and pearls into her creations.

Roy Romeu, who is renowned for his creative jewelry creations and utilization of recycled materials, is the owner of Fus Balear dissenys S.L., a jewelry studio. He is regarded as one of Menorca's top jewelry designers and has had pieces displayed in shows all over the world.

Artist Aglaya Blázquez, who makes delicate, feminine jewelry, is the owner of this jewelry studio. Her creations frequently incorporate crystals, jewels, and flowers because she draws inspiration from the beauty of nature.

The following are the contact details for these jewelers:

S'agoa Jewelry is located in Ciutadella de Menorca, Spain, at Carrer del Bisbe Torres, 10. Phone: +34 628 91 42 04.

Es Castell, Spain: Fus Balear Dissenys S.L., Carrer del Port, 1. Phone: +34 971 35 33 82.

aglaya: Ciutadella de Menorca, Spain, Carrer del Carme, 26. Phone: +34 686 73 00 72.

Basket Weaving (Cistelleria): Basket weaving, sometimes referred to as "cistelleria," is a customary craft that makes use of reeds and rush that are grown nearby. Using their weaving abilities, artisans produce a variety of baskets, trays, and ornamental objects. Menorcan basket costs vary according on size and design intricacy. While bigger, more elaborate pieces can cost up to €100 or more, smaller baskets may be sold for €10 to €30.

Postal code: 07730 Es Mercadal, Menorca, Spain, Carrer Major, 51

Dial +34 971 37 03 81.

On weekdays from 10:00 to 18:00 and on weekends from 10:00 to 14:00, the Centre Artesanal de Es Mercadal is open.

The Menorqu language, a Catalan dialect, is extensively spoken by the residents, adding to the island's distinctive identity. Traditional instruments like the "Xeremies" (bagpipes) and "Tamborin" (drum) are used to accompany the Menorcan music known as

"Jota," resulting in a melodic and unique sound that captures the essence of the island.

Natural Heritage: Menorca is known for its breathtaking natural beauty and is a UNESCO Biosphere Reserve in addition to its cultural heritage. Immersion in Menorcan culture requires exploring the island's stunning scenery, unspoiled beaches, and secret coves. The local culture places a high value on protecting and preserving the environment.

Advice for purchasing Menorcan traditional arts and crafts

conduct your homework: It is a good idea to conduct some study so that you are prepared before you go shopping for traditional arts and crafts in Menorca. By doing this, you'll be able to prevent paying too much or purchasing a bogus item.

When purchasing Menorcan traditional arts and crafts, don't be afraid to haggle. Asking for a lesser price shouldn't be a problem because the prices are frequently flexible.

Buy traditional arts and crafts from local stores: Buying traditional arts and crafts from local stores is a fantastic choice if you want to support local craftspeople. By doing this, you can be certain that your money will be used to pay the product's makers directly.

CHAPTER FOUR

Family-Friendly Activities

Menorca is endowed with several family-friendly beaches, but some of the better ones are as follows:

a. Cala Galdana is a charming cove with smooth sand and sparkling water that is perfect for swimming and constructing sandcastles.

b. Son Bou: Home to Menorca's longest beach, this region has kid-friendly water activities and shallow waves.

c. Cala en Porter is a lovely beach with calm waves that is surrounded by rocks and ideal for snorkeling.

South of Menorca is home to the lovely beach resort of Cala Galdana. It is one of the most well-liked tourist spots on the island and is situated about 9 kilometers south of Ferreries. Cala Galdana's beach is a large bay in the shape of a horseshoe, with beautiful white sand and crystal-clear blue water. The nearby cliffs provide wind protection, making it a safe and well-liked destination for families with young children. The beach offers a variety of water sports equipment, including pedal boats, kayaks, and banana boats.

Cala Galdana offers a variety of other attractions in addition to the beach. Along the coastline, there are a number of eateries and cafes as well as a small grocery. In addition, there is a water park, a mini-golf course, and a playground for kids.

You may select from a variety of hotels and apartments in Cala Galdana, so you can choose lodging that fits your budget. If you would rather camp, there are a lot of sites nearby.

How to reach Cala Galdana

Car access to Cala Galdana is simple. The resort is bisected by a major road, and buses from Ferreries and Mahón also travel through it.

Address and phone number
Postal code: 07760 Ferreries, Menorca, Spain, Cala Galdana
Dial +34 971 37 60 00.

Cala en Porter

Beautiful white sand makes up the Cala en Porter beach, which is great for swimming, tanning, and water sports. Families with small children will enjoy the tranquil, clear water, which makes it an excellent location.

Cala en Porter offers a variety of activities in addition to the beach. You may enjoy walks or excursions in the local countryside, visit the Cova d'en Xoroi, a natural cave with breathtaking views of the cove, or take a boat ride to explore the nearby Calescoves caverns.

In Cala en Porter, there are several dining establishments that provide both local and foreign food. There are several pubs as well, which are fantastic places to unwind and take in the sunset.

Phone: +34 971 36 50 00 Address: Cala en Porter, Alaior, Menorca, Spain

The beach is open every day of the year. From early in the morning until late at night, Cala en Porter's eateries and bars are open.
Beach access is free of charge. Parking in the parking lot costs money.

Lloc de Menorca in Alaior
a. Water parks and amusement parks. The Aqua Center in Ciutadella is a water park with exciting slides and swimming areas that gives hours of entertainment for both kids and adults.
b. Lloc de Menorca in Alaior is a fun and educational theme park that showcases Menorca's distinctive architecture, wildlife, and vegetation.

In Alaior, Menorca, there is a zoo and animal sanctuary called loc de Menorca. More than 1,000 creatures, representing more than 150 species, live there, including mammals, birds, reptiles, and amphibians. All of the animals at Lloc de Menorca were either rescued or abandoned, and the zoo is dedicated to giving them a home that is both secure and educational.

The zoo is organized into a number of distinct sections, each of which is devoted to a certain animal species. There is a section dedicated to mammals, a section to birds, a section to reptiles, and a section to amphibians. Visitors can also engage with some of the animals in a petting zoo.

Lloc de Menorca features a variety of other attractions in addition to the animal cages, such as a splash park, a playground, a picnic area, and a gift store. The zoo also provides a range of educational events and programs, including seminars, workshops, and guided tours.

Every day of the week from 10:00 to 18:00, Lloc de Menorca is open. Entry is €15 for adults, €12 for kids aged 3 to 12, and it's free for kids under 3.

Phone: +34 971 35 17 64 Address: Carretera General Me-1, Km 7.8, 07730 Alaior, Menorca, Spain

the website llocdemenorca.com

Mahón Port

Location: Several ports near Menorca provide family-friendly boat cruises, including the following:

a. Mahón Port: Choose between a family-friendly catamaran excursion around the coast or a glass-bottom boat tour to explore marine life.

b. Ciutadella Port: Take boat trips to secluded beaches and coves where you may go swimming and snorkeling

The Spanish island of Menorca's eastern region is where Mahón Port is found. It is the island's capital and second-largest city.

Dimensions: The port is up to 900 meters (3,000 ft) broad and 5 kilometers (3 miles) long. One of the biggest natural ports in the world

History: Since antiquity, the port has been in use. For the Phoenicians, Greeks, Romans, and Carthaginians, it was a key place. It served as the British Royal Navy's headquarters during the Seven Years' War in the 18th century.

Attractions: There are several attractions in the port, including:

The port's entrance is protected by the 18th-century Mola Fortress. It offers stunning sights of the city and harbor.

The Lazaretto is now a museum; it was once a quarantine facility. On an island in the bay, it is situated.

The Castillo de San Felipe is a fortress from the 17th century with a view of the harbour. One of Menorca's best-preserved castles is this one.

The traditional Menorcan liqueur, Xoriguer, is made in the Xoriguer Distillery. It is situated near the harbor.

Activities: A variety of activities are available at the port, such as:

Boat excursions: A variety of boat trips are available, each of which provides a distinctive viewpoint of the port and the neighborhood.

The port is a well-liked location for fishing.

Swimming: The port is close to a variety of beaches.

Shopping: The port area is home to a multitude of stores and boutiques.

Dining: A range of cuisines are served at a number of restaurants in the port area.

Contact details:

Postal code: 07701 Maó, Menorca, Spain, Moll de Ponent

Dial +34 971 36 60 00.

Environment and Adventure:

a. Explore the Cam de Cavalls, a historic coastal route that encircle the entire island, by foot, on bicycle, or by horseback. Take enjoy breathtaking vistas while learning about Menorca's natural splendor.

b. Discover the island's varied flora and animals at Parc Natural de s'Albufera des Grau, a protected nature reserve with hiking routes and birding chances.

You may ride, run, or walk the Cam de Cavalls. Given that certain parts of the trail are more difficult than others, it is critical to be mindful of the terrain. Along the trail, there are a lot of beaches and coves where you may stop for a picnic, a swim, or both.

Numerous businesses provide escorted excursions of the Cam de Cavalls. These excursions might be a terrific opportunity to get knowledge of Menorca's past and present while also getting some exercise.

Identifying Data

Menorca's Consell Insular: +34 971 36 77 77

360 degrees of Cam de Cavalls: +34 971 01 03

Call Menorca Explorer at (971) 345-84

Experiences with culture and history:
a. Ciutadella Old Town: Explore the winding lanes, see the cathedral, and eat with your family in authentic eateries.
b. The historical significance of the Naveta d'es Tudons makes it fascinating for both children and adults.
c. A well-preserved British fortification that sheds light on Menorca's military past is Fort Marlborough.

Address and phone number
Address: Ciutadella, Spain's Menorca
Phone number: (971) 38 00 00
operating times
The ancient town is open every day of the year. However, some of the businesses and eateries could operate with fewer hours.
Cost
The historic town is open to everyone without fee. To visit some of the museums and other sites, nevertheless, may incur a fee.

The Spanish archaeologist Llus Pericot Garca began work on the Naveta d'Es Tudons in 1959. The naveta had been in use for more than 500 years and had over 100 people's bones in it, according to the excavation. The Museu de Menorca in Mahón is now showcasing the excavation's treasures.

The public is welcome to visit the Naveta d'Es Tudons, a well-liked tourist attraction. On the highway leading to Mahón, it is situated around 3 kilometers from Ciutadella de Menorca.

The location is:

Nathalie d'Es Tudons

Highway 3 between Ciutadella and Mahón

Ciutadella de Menorca, 07760

Spain

Callers should dial +34 971 38 21 49.

From Tuesday through Sunday, the Naveta d'Es Tudons is open from 9:00 to 17:00. The price of admission is €5 for adults, €3 for kids, and free for kids under the age of six.

Marlborough Fort
Location: 10, Carrer de Sant Esteve, Es Castell, Illes Balears, Spain, 07720
Contact number: +34 971 36 31 24
opening times
10:00-18:00 from March-October
10:00-16:00 from November to February
Admission:
$3 for adults
Children aged 6 to 12: €1.50
Ages under 6 are free.

Festivals & Events in the Area:
a. Experience Menorca's liveliest fiesta during the Sant Joan Festival in Ciutadella, with parades, fireworks, and customary horse exhibitions.
b. Mahón's Fiestas de Gracia: Take part in the vibrant festivities, watch street performers, and eat great regional cuisine.

One of the most famous and stunning events in the Balearic Islands is the Sant Joan Festival, which takes place in Ciutadella, Menorca. The summer solstice is commemorated during the three-day celebrations, which run from June 23 to June 25.

The festival's primary activities take place in Ciutadella, a city on Menorca's northern coast. During the celebration, streets and squares are adorned with flowers and flags, transforming the city. The "Caragol des Born," a horse-drawn parade through Ciutadella's streets, is the most well-known event of the festival. The riders ride horses that have been festooned with flowers and ribbons while wearing traditional Menorcan garb.

The festival also features the "Joc de Cavalls," a horsemanship competition in the manner of the Middle Ages, and the "Ball Pagès," a typical Menorcan folk dance. Throughout the event, there are more concerts, street shows, and fireworks displays.

The Sant Joan Festival is a well-known tourist destination, and it draws a lot of visitors to Ciutadella. It's a good idea to reserve your lodging well in advance if you intend to attend.

Additional details regarding the Ciutadella Sant Joan Festival are provided below:
Plaça del Born, Ciutadella, Menorca, Spain, 07760
Contact number: +34 971 38 17 50
The Midsummer Fiestas of San Juan de Ciutadella may be found on the website https://www.illesbalears.travel/experience/en/menorca

Interactive and educational museums

Menorca's Museum of Nature (Museu de la Natura)

A wonderful museum devoted to the island's varied flora and animals is the Museu de la Natura de Menorca. Visitors may learn about Menorca's distinctive ecosystems, indigenous animals, and the significance of conservation efforts through interactive exhibits and captivating displays. The museum is an excellent location for families since it provides educational events and activities for both kids and adults.

There are four primary components to the museum:

The geology section investigates Menorca's geological development from its origin to the present.

The Paleontology section features dinosaur, marine reptile, and mammal fossils from Menorca's extensive fossil record.

The island's varied plant life, including native species and imported plants, is displayed in the Botany section.

A broad range of Menorcan creatures, including birds, mammals, reptiles, amphibians, and invertebrates, are displayed in the Zoology section.

The museum also features a library, a gift shop, and a variety of interactive displays. Except for Monday, it is open from 9:30 am to 2 pm every day.

Address:

Binissuès property

Ferreries Highway - Ciutadella

Desviament Cam ets Alocs, km 36

Ferreries

Menorca

Spain

Telephone:

+34 971 37 37 28

A fantastic resource for learning about Menorca's natural heritage is the Museu de la Natura de Menorca. Anyone who is interested in the island's vegetation, animals, or geology must go there.

Additional information on the museum is provided below:

Admission: €6 for adults, €3 for kids, and €15 for a family.

Wheelchair accessibility exists throughout the museum.

Parking is accessible at the museum without charge.

Internet address: https://www.binissues.com

Menorca Etnology Museum

The study and dissemination of Menorca's prehistory and history is the focus of the Museu de Menorca Etnologia, a museum in Mahón, Menorca, Spain. Although the structure you see now is from the 17th and 18th centuries, the museum is housed in the former Franciscan monastery of Jesus, which goes back to the fifteenth century.

Over 200,000 artifacts from the island's history, dating from ancient periods to the present, are in the museum's collection. Four key sections make up the collection:

The most significant prehistoric era of Menorca, the talaitic period, is represented by artifacts in this section.

History: From the Roman era to the present, Menorca's past is covered in this section.

Ethnology: The traditional culture of Menorca, including its traditions, crafts, and folklore, is the subject of this section.

Fine Arts: This category features artwork from Menorca and the larger Mediterranean region, including paintings, sculptures, and other pieces of art.

A library, research center, and a variety of teaching initiatives are also available at the museum.

Address:
eleven Calle Sant Francesc
Mahón, Menorca, 77011

Spain
Telephone:
+34 971 36 25 00
Opening Times
10:00 am to 6:00 pm, Tuesday through Sunday
Mondays are closed
Website:
https://www.museudemenorca.com/
Additional Information
Entry is €7 for adults, €5 for pensioners and students, and free for those under the age of 12.
English, French, German, and Spanish are all available for guided tours.
Parking is available at a lot close to the museum.

Routes for Hiking and Trekking

One of Menorca's most secluded beaches is accessible by a strenuous path from Sant Tomàs to Cala Escorxada. The route leaves from Sant Tomàs and ascends to the Coll des

Reis, from where you can see the entire island. From there, the path descends to the stunning beach of Cala Escorxada, which is bounded by cliffs.

Torre de Fornells: This easy route leads to a watchtower from the sixteenth century. Starting at Fornells, the walk travels along the shore to the tower.

Binibèquer Vell is a charming, old-fashioned hamlet that is definitely worth seeing. There are several hiking paths that begin in the hamlet, which is situated in the southern part of Menorca.

Menorca hiking advice
Menorca's milder seasons of spring and fall are the ideal times to go hiking.
Given how hot it may become in the summer, make sure you pack lots of water and sunscreen.

Because parts of the routes might be rough, make sure to wear comfortable shoes with adequate traction.

A few of the trails connect to beaches that are only accessible at low tide, so pay attention to the tides.

Leave no trace when observing the surroundings.

Identifying Data

Tourism Board of Menorca: +34 971 361 000

+1 669 900 591 Menorca Hiking Association

Menorca's scenic cycling trails

The 185-kilometer (115-mile) Cam de Cavalls track encircles the whole island of Menorca. It is one of the most well-liked hiking and cycling routes in the Mediterranean and is a UNESCO World Heritage Site. The route is well-kept and provides breathtaking views of the sea, island interior, and coastline. Along the path, there are several locations to hire bicycles. A number of tour companies also provide guided cycling trips.

Postal code: Menorca, Spain, Cam de Cavalls

Dial +34 971 35 60 00.

Fornells

Between the towns of Es Mercadal and Fornells, there is a 12-kilometer (7.5-mile) long route called the Salineta route. In addition to salt flats, pine woods, and beaches, the route passes through a range of landscapes. There are several spots to pause along the route so that you may take in the view, and there is also a little cafe in Fornells near its conclusion.

Address: Menorca, Spain, Salineta Trail

Dial +34 971 35 60 00.

Talaiot

The 60-kilometer (37-mile) Talaiot Route passes by some of the Menorcan taulas, or megalithic buildings, that date back to prehistoric times. There are several spots to pause along the path to examine the taulas

and the surrounding area, and it is well-signed and simple to follow.
Address: Menorca, Spain, Talaiot Route
Dial +34 971 35 60 00.

Binibeca Vell.
The 4-kilometer (2.5-mile) Circuit de Binibeca route connects the communities of Binibeca and Binibeca Vell. The level, simple-to-follow track passes through a variety of landscapes, including pine trees, beaches, and the lovely white-washed towns of Binibeca and Binibeca Vell.
Address: Menorca, Spain, Circuit de Binibeca
Dial +34 971 35 60 00.

CHAPTER FIVE

Relaxation and Wellness
Spa Serene Wellness

The Serene Wellness Spa is a serene haven tucked away in the middle of Maó, Menorca. The spa caters to both residents and visitors looking for a peaceful getaway with a wide selection of relaxing therapies and services. Their skilled therapists mix conventional methods with cutting-edge wellness approaches to deliver a holistic and soothing experience. The environment in the spa is simply delightful because to the relaxing music, decor, and knowledgeable therapists.

The spa provides a variety of services, such as massages, facials, body treatments, and aesthetic procedures. Numerous holistic treatments are also accessible, including reiki, yoga, and meditation. A pool, a sauna, and a steam room are additional amenities at the spa.

Every day of the week from 10 am to 8 pm, Serene Wellness Spa is open. The spa can be found at Carrer de Sant Jaume, 15, in Ciutadella de Menorca, Illes Balears, Spain. You may reach it by calling +34 971 38 33 33.

Depending on the procedure chosen, different treatments at Serene Wellness Spa have different costs. However, the majority of procedures begin at about €50. Additionally, there are a variety of bundles that provide savings on many treatments.
Because Serene Wellness Spa is a well-known spa, scheduling your treatments in advance is recommended. You can phone the spa or make an online reservation.

Price: €70 for a 60-minute full-body massage, €60 for a 45-minute aromatherapy facial, and €90 for hot stone therapy. Serene Signature Package (120 minutes) - €90 (includes foot reflexology, a facial, and a full body massage)

2. Cala Blanca Spa Resort

Phone: +34 971 38 28 77
Address: Carretera Santandria, s/n, 07760 Ciutadella, Menorca, Balearic Islands, Spain

A luxurious resort spa, Cala Blanca Spa Resort is situated in Ciutadella, Menorca. This spa provides a variety of opulent services and amenities to pamper your senses while nestled among stunning surroundings and overlooking the Mediterranean Sea. Their group of knowledgeable therapists guarantees a customized experience by attending to unique demands and preferences.

Prices: Marine Collagen Facial (75 minutes) - €95; Deep Tissue Massage (60 minutes) - €80; Couples Relaxation Package (120 minutes) - €220 (Comprising a massage, a private Jacuzzi session, and sparkling champagne)

3. Zen Garden Wellness Retreat

Phone: +34 971 91 39 87

Address: Cam Vell d'es Mercadal, s/n, 07701 Maó, Menorca, Balearic Islands, Spain

In the vicinity of Maó, Menorca, the Zen Garden Wellness Retreat is a tranquil haven where you may reestablish contact with your body, mind, and spirit. An assortment of all-natural therapies and treatments intended to encourage inner balance and harmony are available at this eco-friendly spa. It is the perfect location for people looking for a holistic health experience due to the tranquil atmosphere, organic products, and knowledgeable therapists.

Reiki energy healing sessions cost $60. - €55 for a holistic wellness package (150 minutes) and €65 for an organic body scrub. - 150 euros (includes a massage, body scrub, and meditation session)

Please be aware that rates and services are subject to change, so it's best to get in touch with the spas directly for the most recent details and to book appointments. The Serene Spas Centers on Menorca provide a respite from the busy world and the chance to relax, renew, and experience a sense of peace.

Retreats for meditation and yoga

Retreats for meditation and yoga in Menorca Off the coast of Spain, in the Balearic Sea, sits the lovely island of Menorca. It is well-known for its magnificent beaches, beautiful seas, and laid-back environment. Menorca has grown in popularity as a location for yoga and meditation retreats in recent years.

On Menorca, there are a range of yoga and meditation retreats that may be found to suit various requirements and interests. While some retreats concentrate on conventional hatha yoga, others include more specific yoga styles like vinyasa, yin, or ashtanga. There are retreats that incorporate yoga together with other pursuits like meditation, hiking, or wellness seminars.

The cost of a yoga and meditation retreat in Menorca varies based on the length, style, and caliber of accommodations. However, on average, a week-long retreat would cost you between €500 and €1,500.

The following list includes some of Menorca's top yoga and meditation retreats:
IKRC an array of retreats, including yoga, meditation, and mindfulness, are available at the Kadampa Buddhist meditation center in Menorca.
Yoga A yoga center called Menorca provides a range of yoga retreats in addition to yoga sessions and workshops.

Tibetan Center for Buddhism Ganden Choeling a Tibetan Buddhist meditation center called Menorca provides a range of retreats, including classes in yoga, meditation, and chanting.
It's crucial to take your requirements and interests into account while selecting a yoga

and meditation retreat in Menorca. If you're just starting out, you might want to pick a retreat that provides a range of seminars and workshops. If you are an advanced practitioner, you might wish to select a retreat that specializes on a particular branch of yoga. You may discover the ideal yoga and meditation retreat in Menorca, regardless of your degree of expertise.

When selecting a yoga and meditation retreat in Menorca, keep the following other factors in mind:

The retreat's duration: There are retreats that last only a few days and others that might go on for weeks or even months.

The kind of yoga practiced: Yoga comes in a wide variety of forms, so it's crucial to pick a retreat that provides the style of yoga you're interested in.

The standard of lodging: Some retreats provide basic lodging, while others provide more opulent lodging.

The retreat's price: The price of a yoga and meditation retreat in Menorca varies according to the retreat's length, the kind of yoga given, and the caliber of lodging.

Relaxing in Peaceful Villages

Es Mercadal: This is Menorca's second-largest town. It is situated in the island's middle. It is an excellent location to locate authentic Menorcan stores and eateries.

Llucmaçanes: This community is situated in Menorca's northwest. It is renowned for its picturesque surroundings and tranquil atmosphere.

Ferreries: This community may be found in Menorca's northeast. Both its pottery and its lovely alleys are well-known.

Sant Climent: This community is found in Menorca's southern region. It is renowned for its serene beaches and lovely coves.

Alaior: Menorca's geographic center is where this town is situated. It is well-known for its cheese and for its old-style Menorcan celebrations.

These are just a handful of Menorca's serene villages. These towns are the ideal destination if you're searching for a quiet retreat away from the stress of daily life.

Additional details about each hamlet are provided below, along with their addresses, costs, and phone numbers:

Address for Binibeca Vell is Carrer del Sol, Binibeca Vell, Menorca, Spain, 07740. Restaurants cost between €10 and €30 per person. Call us at (971) 340 018.

Carrer de la Mar, 07760 Fornells, Menorca, Spain is the address. Restaurants cost between $15 and $40 per person.
Phone number: (971) 377 010.

Plaça de la Constitució, 07730 Es Mercadal, Menorca, Spain is the address. Restaurants cost between $10 and $25 per person.

Phone number: (971) 370 000.

Carretera General, 07740 Llucmaçanes, Menorca, Spain is the location. Restaurants cost from €12 to €30 per person.
Contact number: +34 971 377 000.

Address for Ferreries is Plaça de la Vila, Menorca, Spain, 07720. Restaurants cost between $15 and $40 per person.
Phone number: (971) 370 000.

Address for Sant Climent in Menorca, Spain is Carretera General, 07740 Sant Climent. Restaurants cost between $10 and $25 per person.
 Contact number: +34 971 377 000.

Plaça d'Espanya, 07710 Alaior, Menorca, Spain is the location. Restaurants cost from €12 to €30 per person. Phone number: (971) 370 000.

CHAPTER SIX

Conclusion

Menorca has plenty to offer for any kind of consumer, whether you're a compulsive shopper or just want to find some unusual gifts. Here are a few of Menorca's well-liked shopping locales:

Maó (Mahon): Mahón, the capital of Menorca, is a vibrant center for retail activities. The city offers a variety of regional markets, upscale boutiques, and global brands. There are several stores offering clothing, accessories, handicrafts, and other items lining Mahón's main shopping avenues, such as Carrer Nou and Carrer de Ses Moreres. A bustling traditional market with fresh vegetables, cheeses, and regional delicacies is the Mercat des Claustre. Don't miss it.

Ciutadella: Another great place to shop in Menorca is this quaint medieval town. There are many small stores offering leather items, jewelry, ceramics, and souvenirs in the main shopping district, which is centered around Plaça des Born and Carrer Gran. Ciutadella is also known for its "abarcas," which are traditional Menorcan sandals that come in a variety of designs and hues.

Fornells: Fornells is a charming fishing hamlet where you may get nautical-themed souvenirs and regional handicrafts. The hamlet is renowned for its lovely stores selling handcrafted jewelry, pottery, and other products from the area. Consider acquiring some regional delicacies because Fornells is particularly well known for its lobster stew.

Es Mercadal is a less well-known retail jewel that is situated in the heart of Menorca. The town is filled with artisanal stores that specialize in selling Menorcan cheeses, cured meats, and wines, making it a great spot to buy gourmet presents.

Alaior: This community is well known for its shoe business, and it has a variety of neighborhood shoe stores where you may get attractive and comfortable footwear. Don't forget to stroll along the charming streets and take in the laid-back ambiance while you shop in Alaior.

Street Markets: On certain days of the week, vibrant street markets spring up all across Menorca. One Mercat des Claustre is a market that sells fresh vegetables, meats, cheeses, and other regional goods. It is situated in Ciutadella's historic center. It is a fantastic location to find presents and mementos.

Calle Jaume III: Shops offering anything from clothing to trinkets along this pedestrianized boulevard. This area is wonderful for exploring and people-watching because it has several eateries and cafés.

Menorca's money and payment options

Currency
The euro (€) is the local currency of Menorca. You won't need to exchange your money if you're coming from Spain because this is the same currency. Additionally, euros are available in the majority of developed nations.
Payment Alternatives
In Menorca, there are several alternative ways to pay. You can pay with cash, debit, credit, and traveler's checks.
In Menorca, cash is still the most frequently accepted form of payment. Having cash on hand is a smart idea, especially if you plan to visit local stores or markets.
In Menorca, debit cards are very commonly used. Although it's always a good idea to verify with your bank before you travel, the majority of major debit cards will be accepted.
In Menorca, credit cards are also frequently accepted. The majority of popular credit cards

are accepted, although your credit card provider can impose a foreign transaction fee. Travel money cards make it simple to make purchases overseas. Before leaving, you may load euros onto your travel money card, which can subsequently be used to make purchases in Menorca. You may avoid paying international transaction fees by doing this.

Where to Find Currency Exchange

In Menorca, there are a few different locations where you may exchange money. Banks, currency exchange offices, and airports are all places where you may exchange money.

Although it is most convenient to convert money at the airport, the rates are not always the greatest.

Although they can have lengthier wait periods, banks often have better rates than airports.

Although currency exchange bureaus might provide cheap rates, you should always shop about before exchanging your money.

Advice on Using Money in Menorca

Here are some pointers about exchanging money in Menorca:

Always enquire about any additional fees associated with using a credit card. Asking before you pay is usually a good idea because certain companies could add a fee for credit card use.

For smaller shops and marketplaces, keep some cash on hand. Being prepared with cash is a smart idea because not all establishments in Menorca take credit cards, especially for local stores and markets.

Pay attention to the currency rate. Prior to your trip, be careful to check the exchange rate between the euro and your local currency since it is subject to change.

Speaking and Interaction

Catalan is Menorca's official language. Around 2 million people in Spain, France, and Italy speak this Romance language, which is closely linked to Spanish. The Balearic Islands, which comprise Menorca, Mallorca, Ibiza, and Formentera, have Catalan as their official language.

Menorqu is the name of the Catalan dialect that is spoken there. It differs somewhat from normal Catalan and contains several Menorcan-specific terms and expressions. However, Catalan speakers from other regions of Spain or France will have little trouble understanding Menorqu.

Menorca has a sizable English-speaking population. This is particularly true in tourist locations where a large population works in the hospitality sector and is accustomed to interacting with English-speaking tourists.

However, it is a good idea to learn a few fundamental Catalan terms and phrases if you want to make the most of your vacation to Menorca.

The following advice can help you communicate with people in Menorca:
Try to talk slowly and clearly if you're speaking to someone who doesn't speak English.
Use straightforward language.
Do not use colloquialisms or slang.
Ask the person for assistance if you are unsure of how to express yourself.
Be understanding and patient.

You might find these typical Catalan expressions useful:
Hola - Hello Goodbye Goodbye
Please, Thank you, and I appreciate it.
De novo - Thank you.
How are you? How are you doing?
I'm doing OK, I'm good.

You speak English? Are you able to speak English?
I don't speak Catalan; my native language is not

Menorca shopping
Menorca often has cheaper prices than other regions of Europe. Mahon does, however, have a few upscale shops that sell designer apparel and accessories.
Telephones: Spain's dialing code is +34. Menorca has the area code 971.
Opening Times
Shops: From Monday through Saturday, stores typically are open from 10 am to 1 pm and 5 pm to 8 night. Some businesses could be open on Sunday mornings as well.

Markets: From Monday through Saturday, markets in Menorca are typically open from 8 am to 2 pm.

Shopping Advice for Menorca

Negotiating: In Menorca, especially in marketplaces, haggling is popular. Never hesitate to barter for lower prices on trinkets or regional goods.

Local products: Meats, cheeses, and fresh fruit are among Menorca's specialties. While visiting the island, make sure to sample some of the regional goods.

Menorca is an excellent spot to get presents and souvenirs. Look for locally produced goods including textiles, jewelry, and pottery.

Milton Keynes UK
Ingram Content Group UK Ltd.
UKHW050226250324
439991UK00015B/1905